# Start With This

*The Step-by-Step System to Take Control of Your Money, Save More, and Build Real Wealth—Even If You're Starting From Scratch*

REGINE GODEFROY
AUTHOR

*THE JOURNEY BEGINS with ...*

## 📃 Copyright

**Start With This: The Step-by-Step System to Take Control of Your Money, Save More, and Build Real Wealth—Even If You're Starting From Scratch**



Published by ShopUnlocked LLC

ISBN: 978-1-968744-00-7



This publication is for informational purposes only and is not intended to serve as financial, legal, or investment advice. The author and publisher make no guarantees regarding financial outcomes.

All product names, logos, and brands are property of their respective owners. Their use does not imply affiliation with or endorsement by them.

**Printed in the United States of America**

First Edition, 2025

To request permission, contact:

📧 support@shopunlocked.com

🌐 www.shopunlocked.com

*Facing the mirror ...*

**Dedicated to every person who's ever felt overwhelmed by money**

**—but chose to try again anyway.**

rg.
REGINE GODEFROY
AUTHOR

*From Chaos to Clarity ...*

*Planting The Seed of Wealth !*

Wealth doesn't begin with money
— it begins with belief and one bold step.

# Table of Contents

PREFACE

# Why I Wrote This Book

I didn't grow up knowing how to manage money.

Like most people, I had to figure it out the hard way—with mistakes, pressure, and no roadmap.

I wasn't born into wealth, and I didn't have a finance degree.

What I had was discipline, vision, and the belief that I didn't have to stay stuck. I studied, practiced, failed, restarted—and eventually, I built my life back up. That journey inspired this book.

This is the book I wish I had when I was starting out.

You don't need perfection. You just need a plan.

That's what you'll find here: clear steps, encouragement, and tools that actually work. Not just to save money

**— but to feel powerful with it.**

If you've ever felt overwhelmed by money, this book is your fresh start.

It's also the first in a 4-part series. Once you finish this one, you'll be ready for the next steps: fixing your credit, getting out of debt, and building wealth.

And if no one else has told you this yet—**you can do it. You're not too late. And you're not alone.**

Welcome to your journey.

rg.
REGINE GODEFROY
AUTHOR

*Founder of Shopunlocked*
*www.shopunlocked.com*

CHAPTER 1

# Welcome to Your Money Journey

> *"Money is a tool. When you learn how to use it, you build your future—not just survive it."*

Welcome,

You're here for a reason. Whether you're a student trying to pay your way through school, a single mom looking for financial stability, a wife tired of relying on her husband's paycheck, or someone who just arrived in a new country and is facing the American financial system for the first time—this book is your reset button.

It doesn't matter how much money you make, or if you've never had a steady income before. What matters is what you do with your money, starting now.

If you've ever felt frustrated, confused, or ashamed about how you handle your money, let this be the moment you decide to change things. You're not behind. You're not broken. You just haven't had the right tools—until now.

This chapter is the beginning of your journey from financial frustration to confidence. Let's take a good look at where you are, why it matters, and where you want to go.

## The Cost of Doing Nothing

Most people don't take money seriously until it becomes a crisis. Especially in immigrant households or among young people, it's easy to grow up seeing parents pay bills, buy groceries, send remittances, and still say,

> *"Everything's gonna be fine."*

But here's the truth: most of the time, it's not fine. It's hard. It takes strategy, discipline, and hard choices. No one hands us a magic wand. No one is coming to save us. And hoping it all works out — well, that's not a strategy.

❌ Missed opportunities to save or grow

❌ Debt that quietly gets worse

❌ Long nights of worry and financial arguments

❌ Delayed dreams, postponed goals, emotional burnout

> *"If you grew up thinking money will always somehow show up, you're not alone. But in real life, money follows effort, not hope."*

This book is your blueprint. If you're a dad who suddenly became a single parent, or a young woman realizing you want independence, or a college student figuring things out alone—you are not alone in this. And you don't have to stay overwhelmed.

This is your shift.

## Understanding the Real Role of Money

Most people believe money is just something you earn, spend, or save if you're lucky. But the truth is, money is a tool — and when you learn to manage it with intention, it becomes your partner in creating the life you want.

This isn't about becoming a millionaire overnight. It's about understanding the flow of money in your life and making it work for you instead of against you.

Money touches every part of your day — from the food you eat, the gas in your car, to the stress you feel when unexpected expenses hit. You deserve to feel in control, not confused or afraid.

Let's make this simple.

## Money In, Money Out

The foundation of any financial plan comes down to two key questions:

1. How much money is coming in? *(That's your income)*
2. How much money is going out? *(That's your expenses)*

You don't need to overcomplicate this. Your income is every dollar you receive — paycheck, child support, side hustle, or gift. Your expenses are anything you spend — rent, groceries, Netflix, or that "one-time" Amazon purchase.

Too many people avoid looking at their numbers because they're scared of what they'll see. But avoiding your money doesn't make the problem go away — it just delays your peace.

**Start tracking. Start paying attention. Clarity is power.**

## The Money Jar Example

Imagine you have a jar. Every time you get paid, you put your money into this jar. Then, you take money out to pay for food, bills, clothes, transportation, and fun.

If more is going out than what's going in, the jar empties fast. If you don't track what's going out, you won't know when you're about to run out.

It's not about earning more first — it's about controlling what you already have.

## Why Most People Struggle

Most people were never taught how to manage money. They learned by watching their parents, friends, or TikTok influencers. Some grew up with fear around money, others with shame. And many believe budgeting is for people who are already rich — when in fact, it's how people *become* rich.

### Let's reset that thinking:

- You're not bad with money
  — **you've just never been shown how to use it well.**
- Budgeting isn't restriction
  — **it's direction**.

- Saving isn't punishment
  — **it's preparation**.
- Being broke isn't your identity
  — **it's a temporary season**.

## Why You Need a Plan

Winging it doesn't work forever. Life is too unpredictable. Without a plan, your money disappears
— and so do your goals.

This book is about helping you create a simple plan that fits your life, your culture, and your dreams. No jargon. No judgment. Just results.

And we'll start by understanding your own money story
— how you think, feel, and behave with money today —
so you can build a better tomorrow.

## What Wealth Really Means

When you hear "wealth," do you picture millionaires and luxury cars? That's not the kind of wealth we're talking about here.

### Real wealth is:

💡 *You can totally write in here. Scribble away like it's your personal money journal!*

- Not checking your bank account before buying groceries

- Sleeping peacefully because you have an emergency fund
- Being able to help a friend or family member without going broke
- Saying YES to your kid's school trip without worry
- Having **peace of mind and serenity**, even if you don't earn six figures
- Add Your Version of Wealth here:

________________________________________

________________________________________

________________________________________

Wealth isn't about flexing—it's about **freedom, security, and rest.**

> *Funny but true: "Financial peace feels better than any pair of designer shoes."*

💡 *Want to reflect deeper? Download the printable and write your own wealth vision. Frame it if you want—this is your blueprint!*
*https://shopunlocked.com/downloads/wealth-vision/*

## 📄 Worksheet: What's Your Money Story?

*(Fill in the blanks below or scan the QR code to complete online)*

1. What's your earliest memory of money?

________________________________________

________________________________________

2. What did money feel like growing up? (Safe, scarce, confusing, etc.)

________________________________________

________________________________________

3. What's a financial mistake you made and what did you learn?

________________________________________

________________________________________

4. What would "peace with money" look like for you?

________________________________________

________________________________________

5. What's your #1 money goal this year? Why now?

________________________________________

________________________________________

📌 *Come back to this at the end of the book and reflect on what changed.*

## 🗒 In-Book Mini Exercise: Your Money Timeline

Most people have an emotional history with money. Let's explore yours:

Choose the option that feels most like your truth.

**1. First memory of money:**

- ☐ Playing store with pretend bills
- ☐ Watching my parents argue over bills
- ☐ Receiving money for chores or grades
- ☐ Never talked about money at home

**2. When you got your first income:**

- ☐ Still waiting for it!
- ☐ Babysitting or small hustle
- ☐ Part-time job while in school
- ☐ First real job as an adult

**3. First money struggle:**

- ☐ Couldn't pay rent
- ☐ Used credit cards for basic needs
- ☐ Had to borrow from someone
- ☐ Still happening now

**4. When you felt in control:**

- ☐ When I budgeted and stuck to it
- ☐ When I saved up for something big
- ☐ Haven't felt that way yet

### 🗒️ Reflect: What do your answers reveal about your current money mindset?

_______________________________________________

_______________________________________________

_______________________________________________

*✍️ Grab the printable! This worksheet helps you unpack your money beliefs. Trust us, it hits different on paper.*

*https://shopunlocked.com/downloads/money-story/*

### What's Your Financial Personality?

Let's be honest—we all have money habits that follow us like shadows.

## 📄 Financial Personality Quiz

**When you think about money, which behavior feels like you?**

1. **The Spender** – "I deserve it!" ... until the bank says otherwise.
2. **The Saver** – "I feel safer with money in the bank, even if I don't use it."
3. **The Avoider** – "If I don't look at the bill, it's not real."
4. **The Investor** – "Let's make our money work harder than we do."
5. **The Giver** – "I can't say no, even when it costs me."

**Mark your top two:**

- ☐ Spender
- ☐ Saver
- ☐ Avoider
- ☐ Investor
- ☐ Giver

🧠 Understanding your money personality helps you pick the right tools later in this book.

> *Funny but true: "I checked my budget and it said: Try again next month."*

🎯 *Wanna test yourself? Take the quiz online and find out if you're a Saver, Spender, Avoider, or Strategist!*

*https://shopunlocked.com/downloads/financial-personality-quiz/*

## Mindset Reset: From Fear to Confidence

Managing money brings up fear for many people. Let's reset that.

### ❌ Thoughts that hurt us:

- "I'm just not good with money."
- "I'll figure it out later."
- "There's never enough."
- "I'm too broke to budget."

These beliefs lead to:

- Procrastination
- Anxiety
- Debt cycles

- Shame
- Discouragement

☑ **Replace with powerful thoughts:**

- "I am learning. I improve with each step."
- "I can build peace, one dollar at a time."
- "It's okay to start small."
- "I choose clarity over confusion."

*Funny but true: "Budgeting isn't sexy, but being broke is worse."*

*Pro Tip ✨ Expense Tracker Challenge*

**Track every single expense for the next 7 days.**

| Date | Item | Amount | Importance | Frequency |
|---|---|---|---|---|
| | | | VL - L - SI - I - VI | Temp Monthly Yearly |
| | | | | |
| | | | | |
| | | | | |
| | | | | |
| | | | | |
| | | | | |
| | | | | |

VL = Very Low | L = Low | SI = Somewhat Important | I = Important | VI = Very Important

> 💡 *Use your results to create your first real budget in Chapter 2.*

☑ *Track it to master it! Download your expense tracker, start logging daily, and spot your leaks like a money detective*

*https://shopunlocked.com/downloads/expense-tracker/*

**Real-Life Spotlight: Tyler's Story**

Tyler, 28, worked 3 side hustles: delivering for Uber, designing on Fiverr, and flipping electronics. He made good money, but always felt broke. Once he tracked his spending, he discovered over $400/month was going to random late-night food apps.

He started automating $75/week into savings. Six months later? $2,000 saved and his first vacation ever.

"I didn't need more money. I needed more direction." ✨

## 📓 Journal Prompt: Letter to Future Me

Use this space to write a letter to your future self.

Where do you want to be financially 12 months from now?

What habits will you be proud of?

How will peace of mind show up in your life?

## letter to your future self – Be kind to yourself

*Ready to get personal? Print the journaling page and write your future self a message they'll thank you for.*

*https://shopunlocked.com/downloads/future-letter/*

### Mini Challenge ☑

Create a new notebook or Google Doc, Title it:

**"My Financial Journey"**

Use it to paste your results, write your reflections, and store your action steps.

*Funny but true: "My budget told me to stay home today. I listened."*

📓 *Level up! Download the first cover page of your new journal and start tracking your wins, challenges, and "aha" moments*

*https://shopunlocked.com/downloads/financial-journey/*

## What's Next?

In Chapter 2, we'll break down budgeting in a way that feels real and flexible. This is how you begin building peace—not pressure.

Let's keep going.

### 💡 Wanna Test Yourself?

You've learned the basics — now let's put it to the test!

Take this quick quiz to check how much you've absorbed and how ready you are to apply it.

📲 **Scan the QR code or visit the link to begin.**

✍ Whether you ace it or not, you'll learn something valuable.

Let's go!

**Introduction to Budgeting and Saving Strategies**

This page is left intentionally blank

# CHAPTER 2

# Master Your Money Flow — Budgeting + Saving That Stick

> *"A budget is telling your money where to go instead of wondering where it went." — Dave Ramsey*

Before you can master budgeting, saving, or investing, you need to understand how money actually works in your life. This chapter breaks down the key building blocks that will make every dollar you earn feel more powerful — and every decision you make more intentional.

We're not going to drown in financial jargon here. We're going to get to the point — so you feel confident when you see these words again in real life.

### What Is Personal Finance?

Let's keep it real: personal finance just means how you manage your money.

Not your neighbor's money. Not your boss's money. **Yours.**

Financial freedom doesn't come from guessing. It comes from paying attention.

Your Money Flows in 3 Main Directions:

1. **Income** – This is all the money you bring in. Whether it's from your Paycheck (after taxes), a side hustle or business, government benefits, child support, Gifts or one-time support or birthday money — if it comes in, it's income.

> 💡 *Important: Use your take-home pay — what actually hits your account.*

2. **Expenses** – This is money going out. Rent, groceries, gas, Wi-Fi, Netflix — every bill or swipe counts as an expense.
3. **Savings and Investments** – This is money you *keep* or *grow*. It's the portion you don't spend — and that's where the magic begins.

> 💡 *Quick Tip: The goal is to grow the gap between your income and your expenses — and fill that gap with savings and smart decisions.*

## Definitions That Actually Help You

Let's take these terms out of the textbook and into real life.

### 💸 Income

Money coming in. Whether it's hourly, salaried, part-time, or passive — it's your fuel. More income gives you more flexibility, but managing what you have now is the first step.

### 💳 Expenses

Money going out. Expenses come in two flavors:

- **Fixed Expenses**: Rent, car payment — same amount every month.
- **Variable Expenses**: Groceries, gas, fun — these change monthly.

Tracking your expenses isn't about guilt. It's about clarity.

### 🏦 Budget

A budget is not a punishment. It's a *permission slip* for your money. It tells your dollars where to go — before they disappear.

Your budget should reflect your priorities, your goals, and your life. It's a living, breathing plan — not a cage.

### 💰 Savings

Money set aside for future you. It could be for emergencies, a big goal, or just peace of mind.

Emergency savings = no panic when the car breaks down.

Goal savings = that vacation or business idea finally happens.

Start small. Stay consistent.

### 📈 Investment

When you put money into something that can grow. This could be the stock market, real estate, or your own business.

> 💡 *Reminder: You don't need thousands to start investing — just the right plan and patience.*

### 💵 Assets vs. Liabilities

- **Assets**: Things you own that can grow in value or help you earn more (example: a laptop for work, a home, or a business).
- **Liabilities**: Things you owe money on (example: credit card debt, car loan, unpaid bills).

The goal? Build more assets than liabilities. That's how you grow *net worth.*

### 📊 Net Worth

Net Worth = What You Own – What You Owe

Even if the number is negative right now, tracking it gives you direction. Progress over perfection.

## The 4 Pillars of Financial Wellness

Everything we'll cover in this book sits on top of four key areas:

1. **Earn** – How you bring in money
2. **Spend** – How you use money
3. **Save** – How you hold on to money
4. **Grow** – How you multiply money

Most people get stuck on "earn and spend" and never build the habit of "save and grow." That ends now.

Let's Be Honest About Budgeting

For a lot of people, the word "budget" sounds like punishment. Like it's about cutting out everything fun.

But in real life, a **budget is freedom**. It's your way of saying, "This is what matters to me — and this is how I'll make room for it."

You're not here to penny-pinch every moment of your life. You're here to create peace, gain control, and move forward with purpose.

### Why Most Budgets Fail

Budgets don't fail because you're "bad with money."

They fail because they're either:

- too strict
- too complicated

- or too unrealistic for real people with real lives

Your new budget is going to be flexible, human, and smart. That's how we build habits that stick.

### Money Doesn't Have to Be Complicated

Let's take the mystery out of money. Financial basics are not about being perfect — they're about being intentional. You're not "bad with money" if no one ever taught you. That's what this chapter is here for.

### Let's Talk About the Elephant in the Room: Fear

Before we dive into budgets, let's get real. Most of us avoid budgeting because it feels like a mirror we don't want to look into. We're afraid it will tell us that we can't afford the life we want. That we need to downgrade. That we need to say no to things that make us feel good.

**We fear:**

- Looking broke to our friends
- Saying no to our kids
- Admitting we need help
- Facing how much we waste without realizing it

But here's the truth:

**A budget doesn't take away your freedom. It gives it back to you.**

Budgeting is how we break cycles. Whether you grew up watching your parents live paycheck to paycheck or you're just now realizing money doesn't stretch on its own—this chapter will show you how to give your money direction.

**What's Your Budget Style?**

Just like your money story and your financial personality, your budget should fit your life. Here are three budget styles and who they work best for:

## The 50-30-20 Rule

50% Needs / 30% Wants / 20% Savings or Debt

**Great for:** Beginners, people with steady income

**Example:**

- Monthly income: $2,000
- Needs (rent, bills): $1,000
- Wants (eating out, shopping): $600
- Savings/Debt: $400

> 📊 *Time to test the rule! Use the printable to plug in your numbers and see where your money really goes.*
>
> *https://shopunlocked.com/downloads/503020-practice/*

## The Zero-Based Budget

Every dollar has a job. Income – Expenses = Zero

**Great for:** People who like control, irregular income earners

**Example:**

- Monthly income: $2,500
- Rent: $900
- Utilities: $200
- Food: $400
- Transportation: $300
- Savings: $300
- Debt: $200
- Fun: $200

> 📋 *Give every dollar a job. Download this zero-based budget sheet and tell your money exactly where to go.*
>
> *https://shopunlocked.com/downloads/zero-based-budget/*

## The Anti-Budget

Save first, spend the rest freely

**Great for:** People who hate rules, freelance workers

**Example:**

- Monthly income: $2,200
- Save $500 automatically
- Bills: $1,000

Rest is flexible spending

*Keep it chill. If detailed budgeting isn't your thing, try this flow-style anti-budget worksheet. Simpler, but still powerful.*

*https://shopunlocked.com/downloads/anti-budget/*

## 💡 Wanna Test Yourself?

You've learned the basics — now let's put it to the test!

Take this quick quiz to check how much you've absorbed and how ready you are to apply it.

📲 **Scan the QR code or visit the link to begin.**

✍️ Whether you ace it or not, you'll learn something valuable. Let's go!

**Fundamentals of budget creation**

## 🧠 Quiz: What Budget Style Fits Me?

> 💡 *You can totally write in here. Scribble away like it's your personal money journal!*

**1. How do you feel about tracking expenses?**

- ☐ I need structure (Go 50/30/20 style)
- ☐ I love detail (Go Zero-Based style)
- ☐ I hate it (Go Anti-Budget style)

**2. Is your income regular?**

- ☐ Yes (Any style works!)
- ☐ No (Zero-Based or Anti-Budget style)

**3. Do you have savings goals?**

- ☐ Yes, and I want to hit them fast (Zero-Based or Anti-Budget style)

## 📄 Worksheet: My First Budget Draft

| Category | Monthly Amount | Notes |
|---|---|---|
| Housing | | Rent or mortgage |
| Utilities | | Electricity, gas, water |
| Groceries | | Food at home |
| Transportation | | Gas, public transport |
| Insurance | | Car, health, rental |

| | | |
|---|---|---|
| Debt Payments | | Credit cards, loans |
| Savings | | Emergency fund, future goals |
| Fun & Personal | | Dining, hobbies, subscriptions |
| Miscellaneous | | Anything else |
| **TOTAL** | | Make sure total = income |

> ◇ *Tip: Fill this in after doing your 7-day expense tracker from Chapter 1.*

🛠 *Your blueprint starts here! Print your first draft and tweak as you go—this is the foundation of your financial life.*

*https://shopunlocked.com/downloads/budget-draft/*

**Real-Life Spotlight: Vanessa's Pivot**

Vanessa, 35, was a single mom of two working as a CNA. She feared budgeting would expose how behind she was. But after one weekend of writing things down, she saw she could save $150/month just by meal prepping and switching phone plans. She now budgets with her oldest daughter once a week—and they treat it like a game.

"My money isn't perfect, but now I know where it's going. That's power." ✨

## Step-by-Step: Build Your First Budget

### Know your monthly income

*Why:* You can't budget what you don't track.

*Real life:* Use last 3 months' average.

*Time:* 10–15 mins

**How:**

- Grab your **last 3 months of bank statements or pay stubs** (paper or digital).
- Highlight all your income: salary, side hustle, government payments, or family help.
- Add each month's income and divide by 3 to find your average.

**Document to Use:** Bank statements, pay stubs, Zelle/Cash App/PayPal records.

**Tool:** Calculator or spreadsheet.

> 💡 *Important: Use your take-home pay — what actually hits your account.*

## 💡 Wanna Test Yourself?

You've learned the basics — now let's put it to the test!

Take this quick quiz to check how much you've absorbed and how ready you are to apply it.

📲 **Scan the QR code** or **visit the link** to begin.

✍ Whether you ace it or not, you'll learn something valuable. Let's go!

**Creating a Budget Tailored to Your Goals**

## Insert YOUR numbers here:

________________________________________

________________________________________

________________________________________

________________________________________

________________________________________

________________________________________

________________________________________

________________________________________

________________________________________

**➡ Final Answer: My average monthly income is:**
**$**______________

💰 *What's coming in? This sheet helps you calculate your average monthly income, even if it changes each month.*

*https://shopunlocked.com/downloads/monthly-income/*

## List fixed + variable expenses

For one full month, track every dollar that leaves your pocket.

Use a notebook, spreadsheet, or below note lines. Don't overthink it — just write it down.

### Example categories:

- Rent or mortgage
- Groceries
- Utilities (electricity, water, internet)
- Transportation (gas, Uber, bus)
- Debt payments
- Subscriptions
- Fun money
- Giving or donations

You'll be shocked where your money leaks. And once you see it, you can change it

*Why:* See what must stay vs what can adjust.

*Real life:* Rent, bills vs groceries, gas

*Time:* 30 mins

**How:**

Look through your last month's bank/credit card statements.

Write down:

**Fixed:** Rent, car payment, subscriptions, insurance.

**Variable:** Groceries, gas, eating out, gifts.

**Document to Use:** Bank statement or budgeting app.

> **Tip:** *Use different colors or columns for Fixed vs Variable.*

**Example:**

Fixed:

- Rent: $950
- Car Insurance: $150

Variable:

- Groceries: $300
- Eating Out: $125

**Insert your Fixed & Variable expenses here:**

______________________________________________

______________________________________________

______________________________________________

______________________________________________

______________________________________________

➔ **Final Answer: Total Fixed: $________ |**

**Total Variable: $________**

*📋 Control the controllables. Use this template to break down what's set in stone vs. what can flex.*

*https://shopunlocked.com/downloads/fixed-variable-expenses/*

## Categorize wants vs needs

You're not here to suffer.

But you *are* here to get intentional.

- A "need" is something that keeps you alive, safe, and able to work or care for others.
- A "want" is everything else.
    - *Why:* Helps cut wisely
    - *Real life:* Netflix = want, electricity = need
    - *Time:* 15 mins

Your goal isn't to remove joy — just to put joy in the *right place* on your priority list

**How:**

- Go back to your list of expenses.
- For each one, ask: *"Would I survive without this for a month?"*
    - If yes → **Want**
    - If no → **Need**
- For each item, write down how much you **realistically** spend per month.
- Prioritize <u>**needs first**</u>, then distribute what's left to wants or savings.
- Use the **50/30/20 rule** as a guide:

- 50% Needs
- 30% Wants
- 20% Savings or Debt Repayment

**Example (on $2,500 income):**

- Needs (Rent, utilities, food) = $1,250
- Wants (Dining, streaming, shopping) = $750
- Savings/Debt = $500

**Example:**

Netflix = Want

Electricity = Need

Gym Membership = Want

Medication = Need

**Document to Use:** Your Fixed & Variable expenses from Step 2.

**Document to Use:** Budget template below or spreadsheet.

| Category | Planned Amount ($) | Actual Amount ($) | Notes |
|---|---|---|---|
| INCOME | | | |
| Primary Job | | | |
| Side Hustle | | | |
| Other Income | | | |

| | | | |
|---|---|---|---|
| EXPENSES | | | |
| Rent/Mortgage | | | |

| | | | |
|---|---|---|---|
| Utilities (Electricity, Water) | | | |
| Groceries | | | |
| Transportation (Gas, Uber) | | | |
| Phone & Internet | | | |
| Insurance (Health, Car) | | | |
| Debt Payments | | | |
| Savings | | | |
| Entertainment | | | |
| Subscriptions | | | |
| Miscellaneous | | | |
| **TOTALS** | | | |

➡ **Final Answer:**

**My planned spending → Needs: $________________________**

**Wants: $__________________ Savings/Debt: $_______________**

*Need it or want it? Download the worksheet to finally draw the line—and take back your power.*

*https://shopunlocked.com/downloads/wants-needs/*

## Check if it balances

Now that you know your income and expenses, it's time to map out a plan that matches your goals.

Use this simple formula:

**Income – Expenses = What's Left**

*Why:* This makes your budget actionable; Your expenses should not exceed income

> *Tip: Be realistic, not harsh; Adjust until it works*

*Time:* 10 mins

**How:**

- Add up your planned expenses from Step 3.
- Compare with your average income from Step 1.
- If total spending > income → make cuts in wants first, then adjust variable needs.
- If spending < income → great! Assign extra to savings or debt.

**Example:**

Income = $2,500

Total expenses = $2,800 ✗

Revise: Cut $150 from shopping, $100 from dining out.

Now expenses = $2,550 ☑ (Still need $50 adjustment or increase income)

**Document to Use:** Your full budget plan below.

| Category | Planned Amount ($) | Actual Amount ($) | Notes |
|---|---|---|---|
| **PLANNED EXPENSES** | | | |
| **AVERAGE INCOME** | | | |
| | | | |

- If total spending > income → make cuts in wants first, then adjust variable needs.
- If spending < income → great! Assign extra to savings or debt.

**Final Answer: My budget is (check one):**

- ☐ Balanced
- ☐ Needs adjustment by $____________

*Here's your budget on one clean page. Plug in your income, adjust your expenses, and print a fresh one each month.*

*https://shopunlocked.com/downloads/budget-template/*

## Budget Check-In Challenge

Each Sunday this month, ask:

**Did I overspend? Where?**

______________________________________________

______________________________________________

______________________________________________

**What surprised me?**

______________________________________________

______________________________________________

______________________________________________

**What can I adjust?**

______________________________________________

______________________________________________

______________________________________________

**What am I proud of?**

______________________________________________

______________________________________________

______________________________________________

Use a sticky note or Notes app to track this weekly.

> *Funny but true: "I made a budget... then my budget saw my Amazon cart and cried."*

*How's it going? Grab this check-in sheet to review your progress weekly or monthly. Keep your goals front and center!*

*https://shopunlocked.com/downloads/budget-check-in/*

### Bonus: Budget Affirmations

Say these out loud when doubt creeps in:

- "My money has purpose."
- "I'm not broke. I'm building."
- "Budgeting is a skill I'm learning."
- "Peace is better than pressure."

### Take Action: Pay Yourself First

Even if it's just $10 a week, automate a transfer into savings. This teaches your brain:

*"Saving is non-negotiable."*

## ✏ Review and Adjust Monthly

Every month, check what worked, what didn't, and where your money surprised you. Your budget should evolve with your goals.

Common Budgeting Traps to Avoid

❌ Guessing instead of tracking

❌ Forgetting irregular expenses (like annual fees or school supplies)

❌ Using credit cards like income

❌ Thinking budgeting = restriction

❌ Trying to be perfect from Day 1

You don't need to be perfect. You just need to be present.

**What's Next?**

In Chapter 3, we'll explore how to build a savings system that actually sticks—even if you've failed before.

Let's build peace, one dollar at a time.

## Sample Budget Template

Here's a simple layout to follow:

| Category | Budgeted | Actual | Notes |
|---|---|---|---|
| Rent | $____________ | $____________ | Fixed |
| Groceries | $____________ | $____________ | Weekly shopping |
| Utilities | $____________ | $____________ | Internet, electricity, etc |
| Transportation | $____________ | $____________ | Gas/Uber/ Bus |
| Debt Payments | $____________ | $____________ | Credit cards or loans |
| Fun / Personal | $____________ | $____________ | Movies, eating out |
| Giving | $____________ | $____________ | Tithes, support |
| Savings | $____________ | $____________ | Pay Yourself First |
| Add more | | | |
| Add more | | | |
| Add more | | | |

*Funny But True : I started a budget and suddenly my money stopped sneaking out at night."*

CHAPTER 3

# Savings That Stick

*"Saving money isn't about how much you make. It's about how much you keep on purpose."*

## Why Saving Feels Hard (and Why It's Not Your Fault)

Saving money sounds simple, right? "Just put some aside." But when you're juggling rent, bills, school, kids, unexpected repairs, and maybe even sending money back home, it can feel impossible.

**Here's the truth:**

- We were not taught how to save.
- Many of us saw our parents live paycheck to paycheck.
- Most financial advice is full of jargon or guilt.
- We fear that saving means deprivation.

And the worst fear of all? **That saving means admitting we can't afford the life we're pretending to live.**

> *"A budget shows you what's possible. A savings plan shows you what's sustainable."*

Let's start fresh. Saving doesn't mean living like a monk. It means taking back control—one dollar at a time

Just like your money story and budget style, your saving style should match your reality and mindset. Here are three:

### 1. The Autopilot Saver

Best for: Busy people who forget to save.

- **How it works:** Set up automatic transfers each payday into a savings account.
- **Real-life tool:** Use your bank's auto-transfer feature or apps like **Qapital** or **Digit**.
- **Example:** Sara earns $1,200 biweekly. She sets $50 to auto-transfer the day her paycheck hits. Over a year: $1,300 saved without lifting a finger.

### 2. The Visual Goal Saver

Best for: People who need motivation to stay on track.

- **How it works:** Pick a goal (emergency fund, trip, laptop). Set a visual savings chart or jar.
- **Real-life tool:** Use printable trackers, or a chart on your wall.

- **Example:** David wants $600 for a certification course. He prints a chart with 12 boxes of $50 each and colors one every time he saves.

### 3. The Challenge-Based Saver

Best for: Competitive or inconsistent earners.

- **How it works:** Use games or challenges to boost saving.
  - **100 Envelope Challenge:** Label 100 envelopes with numbers 1-100. Randomly choose an envelope and save that amount. Finish all = $5,050 saved.
  - **No-Spend Weeks:** Choose one week a month to spend only on essentials.
  - **Round-Up App:** Apps like Acorns or Chime round up each purchase and save the extra change.

**Sheet: Pick Your Saving Style**

### 1. Which sentence feels most true?

☐ I never remember to save.

☐ I need to SEE my progress to stay motivated.

☐ I love a challenge or goal.

**2. Which saving type seems doable right now?**

☐ Autopilot Saver

☐ Visual Goal Saver

- ☐ Challenge-Based Saver

**3. How much could you realistically save per week?**

- ☐ $5
- ☐ $10
- ☐ $25
- ☐ Other: __________

**Real-Life Spotlight: Marc's Story**

Marc drives Uber and delivers food part-time. His income changes every week. He struggled to save until he started a savings game: Every week, he saved the same amount as his lowest Uber tip.

Some weeks he saved $2. Others, $10. After three months, he had $140 saved—more than he'd ever had in his savings account.

> *"It became a fun game. Now I look forward to it."* ✨

## 🗒 Savings Goal Planner (Worksheet)

**My Top 2 Short-Term Goals (1–6 months):**

1. ______________________________

2. ______________________________

**My Top 2 Long-Term Goals (6+ months):**

1. ______________________________

2. ______________________________

**Target Amount for Goal #1:** $______________________

**Deadline:** ______________________________

**How much can I save weekly?** $____________________

**# of weeks to reach it:** ________________________

## 💭 What Makes Saving Actually Work?

Saving money doesn't just happen because you "know better." It happens when your system fits your life.

Here's what most people don't realize:

- You won't always feel motivated. That's okay.
- You will be tempted. That's normal.
- What matters is the **habit**, not perfection.

The trick? Automate where you can. Make it visible where it helps. And keep it tied to something you care about.

## Short-Term vs Long-Term Savings: Know the Difference

Not all savings serve the same purpose. Let's break them into two:

### ◇ Short-Term Savings

These are things you want to accomplish or protect within 6–12 months:

- Emergency fund
- Holiday gifts
- School fees
- Car maintenance
- Travel plans

You want this money to be **safe and easy to access.** Use a regular savings account or digital envelope.

### ◇ Long-Term Savings

These are bigger dreams that take time:

- Home deposit
- Immigration paperwork
- Starting a business
- Retirement or investing

This money can sit longer and work harder for you — possibly in a high-yield account, CD, or beginner investment account (more in future chapters).

🎯 *Make it visual. Print this and post it somewhere you'll see every day. Watch your goals go from dream to done.*

*https://shopunlocked.com/downloads/savings-goal-planner/*

## Consistency > Amount

Whether you save $5 or $500, it's the act of saving — the habit — that builds momentum.

Even if you feel behind or like it's "not enough," start anyway. Your confidence will grow with every transfer.

### Quick Math

- $5/week = $260/year
- $20/week = $1,040/year
- $50/paycheck = $1,300/year

📌 **Progress is progress. Stay with it.**

### Visual Trick: Name Your Accounts

Instead of just "Savings," rename your bank account labels:

- "My First Emergency Fund"
- "Trip to Dubai"
- "New Business Fund"
- "Laptop for My Side Hustle"

This small change makes a huge difference. It gives your money purpose — and purpose is powerful.

## What If You Fall Off?

Life happens. You might skip a week. Or pull from your savings when you didn't want to. That doesn't mean you failed.

📌 **Just restart. No guilt. No drama.**

**Ask:**

What caused the slip?

---

What would've helped?

---

How can I adjust for next time?

---

This is about building a relationship with your money. One that forgives. One that grows.

---

---

---

---

## 💡 Pro Tips for Making It Stick

- **Name your savings accounts**: “Emergency Fund,” “New Laptop,” or “Dream Trip”
- **Hide your savings account from your online dashboard**
- **Celebrate small wins**: Every $50 milestone counts
- **Use cash envelopes**: Great for visual savers

### 💡 Wanna Test Yourself?

You’ve learned the basics — now let’s put it to the test!

Take this quick quiz to check how much you’ve absorbed and how ready you are to apply it.

📲 **Scan the QR code or visit the link to begin.**

✍️ Whether you ace it or not, you’ll learn something valuable. Let’s go!

**Effective Savings Tactics**

## Journal Prompt: The First Thing I Want to Save For

**Write about:**

- Why this goal matters
- What it will feel like to reach it
- What you're willing to give up (temporarily) to get it

## Quiz: What Type of Saver Are You?

1. When you see a sale:

    ☐ I grab it, even if I don't need it

    ☐ I compare prices, then decide

    ☐ I skip it unless it's a need

2. Your saving strategy is:

    ☐ I don't have one yet

    ☐ Random saving when I can

    ☐ A system I stick to

3. Your biggest obstacle is:

    ☐ Forgetting to save

    ☐ Spending on impulse

    ☐ Not making enough money

🎯 **Results:**

Mostly A = Impulsive Saver

Mostly B = Learning Saver

Mostly C = Strategic Saver

________________________________________

________________________________________

________________________________________

________________________________________

## Challenge ☑ The 30-Day Savings Kickstart

Each week, try one:

- Week 1: Open a separate savings account
- Week 2: Track every small expense
- Week 3: Save your lowest tip/bonus/income
- Week 4: Do a no-spend weekend

Bonus: Repeat next month with higher savings goals.

### ✏ Visual Aid: Sample Savings Chart

*A fun way to track your progress, stay motivated, and see your money grow.*

Use this chart to visually track how much you've saved toward a specific goal. Every time you hit a new milestone, color in the boxes!

| Goal Milestone | Progress Tracker |
|---|---|
| $100 | [▨▨□□□□□□□□] – 10 boxes of $10 each |
| $250 | [▨▨▨□□□□□□□] – 10 boxes of $25 each |
| $500 | [▨▨▨▨▨□□□□□] – 10 boxes of $50 each |

## ☑ How to Use It:

- Print this page or redraw the chart in your notebook.
- Pick your savings goal and match it with the closest chart (or make your own!).
- Color one box every time you hit that dollar amount.
- Celebrate every small win — they add up fast!

📌 *Make it fun!* Use highlighters, stickers, or markers. Keep it where you'll see it often (fridge, bathroom mirror, wallet, etc.).

> ✏ *Color your way to savings. Get your crayons or markers and fill this in as you save. Who said finance isn't fun?*
>
> *https://shopunlocked.com/downloads/visual-progress-tracker/*

### What's Next?

In Chapter 4, we tackle the emergency fund—the foundation of financial peace. You'll learn exactly how much you need, how to build it fast, and how it protects your sanity when life happens.

Let's keep growing.

CHAPTER 4

# Build Your Emergency Fund

> *"Expect the best. Prepare for the worst. Capitalize on what comes." – Zig Ziglar*

## Why You Need an Emergency Fund

Let's be honest—life has a way of surprising us. A job loss, a medical bill, a car repair, or even an emergency trip back home. If you don't have a cushion, one surprise can derail your entire financial progress.

An emergency fund is not a luxury. It's a financial safety net that protects your future, your peace of mind, and your dignity.

> *Funny but true: "Emergencies don't wait for payday."*

☑ **Having even a small emergency fund means:**

- You won't need to borrow money
- You can sleep better at night
- You avoid going further into debt

- You feel in control
- You take back your power

## The Emotional Impact of Emergencies

Emergencies don't just cost money. They cost peace, sleep, and confidence. The stress of scrambling for money can create arguments, delay important decisions, and lead to choices we later regret.

Imagine this:

- Your car won't start, and you're late for work.
- Your child needs urgent dental care.
- Your parent back home needs support, now.
- If you have savings, your first thought isn't panic. It's: "I've got this."

And that confidence is **priceless**.

🧠 Take a deep breath. As you reflect on building your Emergency Fund, what emotions come up? Stress? Guilt? Hope? Write it down. This is your safe space to feel, release, and reset. 🧘

## How Much Do You Need?

**Start small, but aim big.**

Your emergency fund goal depends on your life situation. Use the chart below as a starting point:

| Life Situation | Starting Goal | Long-Term Goal |
|---|---|---|
| Student | $250 | 3 months of rent |
| Single Parent | $500 | 3–6 months expenses |
| Dual-income Household | $1,000 | 3 months combined bills |
| Self-employed/Freelancer | $1,500 | 6 months expenses |

> 💡 *Pro tip: Reaching the first $500 is your main win. Celebrate that!*

▧ *Real Talk:* Some of us come from families where emergencies always meant borrowing. This chapter breaks the cycle.

If the words *Emergency* and *Borrowing* combined trigger something in you — a memory, a fear, a frustration — **pause here**. Write it down below. This is your safe space to unpack it, release it, and rise beyond it. 🧘

________________________________________

________________________________________

________________________________________

## In-Book Exercise: What Could Go Wrong?

Let's be proactive.

**Write down 5 possible emergencies you could face this year:**

> 💡 *You can totally write in here. Scribble away like it's your personal money journal!*

✨ *This isn't to scare you. It's to motivate you.*

Now estimate the cost of each. Then circle the **#1 most likely** and the **#1 most expensive**.

## Where to Keep Your Emergency Fund

**Do not** keep your emergency fund:

✗ In cash under the mattress

✗ In your checking account (you'll spend it)

**Ideal places:**

☑ High-yield savings account (online banks are great)

☑ Separate account at your bank

☑ Credit union with limited access

> *Funny but true: "If it's too easy to access, it's too easy to spend."*

If you're new to online banking, look for accounts with no fees and easy mobile deposit.

> *📌 Pro tip: Connect your savings account to auto-transfer $10 weekly.*

## Worksheet: Emergency Fund Tracker

Use this table to set your goal and track progress.

| Goal Amount | Monthly Contribution | Source of Funds | Completion Date | Notes |
|---|---|---|---|---|
| | | | | |
| | | | | |
| | | | | |
| | | | | |
| | | | | |
| | | | | |
| | | | | |

Update this tracker monthly. Celebrate every milestone!

🚨 *Let's get that cushion in place! Print this tracker and fill in your progress one small win at a time.*

*https://shopunlocked.com/downloads/emergency-fund-tracker/*

## 🗎 Worksheet: Emergency Fund Tracker (Example)

Below is a filled example of how you can use this worksheet to track your emergency fund progress. Adjust the numbers based on your own savings plan.

- My Emergency Fund Goal: $1,000
- Deadline to Reach My Goal: August 31, 2025
- Minimum I can save weekly: $50

### Weekly Savings Progress (Example)

| Week | Date | Amount Saved | Total Saved So Far | Notes (e.g. how you saved it) |
|---|---|---|---|---|
| Week 1 | June 1 | $50 | $50 | Transferred from paycheck |
| Week 2 | June 8 | $60 | $110 | Sold unused item |
| Week 3 | June 15 | $40 | $150 | Saved grocery coupon value |
| Week 4 | June 22 | $50 | $200 | Transferred from paycheck |
| Week 5 | June 29 | $75 | $275 | Bonus from work |
| Week 6 | July 6 | $50 | $325 | Transferred from paycheck |
| Week 7 | July 13 | $55 | $380 | Cut subscription cost |

## ☑ Use your own numbers here:

| Week | Date | Amount Saved | Total Saved So Far | Notes (e.g. how you saved it) |
|---|---|---|---|---|
| | | | | |
| | | | | |
| | | | | |
| | | | | |
| | | | | |
| | | | | |
| | | | | |
| | | | | |
| | | | | |
| | | | | |

*Check in with yourself. This weekly tracker helps you stay consistent—even when life gets chaotic.*

*https://shopunlocked.com/downloads/weekly-savings-progress/*

## Savings Without Sacrifice

You don't need to make huge sacrifices to build an emergency fund. Try these micro-adjustments:

### 1. The $5 Rule:

Every time you get a $5 bill, stash it in a jar. At the end of the month, deposit it (Bank , Credit Union).

**2. Cancel & Redirect:**

Cancel one subscription you barely use. Transfer that amount you usually pay this subscription directly to your emergency fund.

### 3. Side Hustle Boost:

Set a % of side hustle income to go straight into savings.

### 4. Round-Up Apps:

Use apps like Chime, Acorns, or Qapital. Every purchase is rounded up and saved.

💡 **Wanna Test Yourself?**

You've learned the basics — now let's put it to the test!

Take this quick quiz to check how much you've absorbed and how ready you are to apply it.

📲 **Scan the QR code or visit the link to begin.**

✍ Whether you ace it or not, you'll learn something valuable. Let's go!

**Building your emergency fund**

▧ Example: Maria used the Acorns app and saved over $200 in round-ups in just 3 months without noticing a change in her spending.

## Real-Life Story: Naomi's $10 Emergency

Naomi, a single mom, was always broke. She started putting $10 aside from each paycheck—even when it hurt. In 8 months, she saved $320. When her son broke his glasses, she paid cash. No stress, no loans.

> *"It felt small at first, but it turned into power."* ✨

## In-Book Quiz: Emergency Fund Readiness

**Answer Yes or No**:

- ☐ Do you know exactly how much you need to feel safe?
  ☐ Yes ☐ No
- ☐ Do you have a separate savings account for emergencies?
  ☐ Yes ☐ No
- ☐ Do you add to your emergency fund every month?
  ☐ Yes ☐ No
- ☐ Have you used your emergency fund in the past 12 months?
  ☐ Yes ☐ No
- ☐ Do you avoid touching it unless it's urgent? ☐ Yes ☐ No

> 🧠 *Score: Count your "Yes" answers. More than 3? You're on the right track!*

## Challenge: The 60-Day Fund Build

Try this:

- **Week 1–2:** Sell 5 items you don't use. Add all proceeds to your fund.
- **Week 3–4:** Cut 3 "nice but not needed" expenses.
- **Week 5–6:** Add found money (cash gifts, refunds, rebates)
- **Week 7–8:** Take a side hustle and dedicate 100% of the extra to savings.

🚀 Goal: Reach your first $250–$500 in 60 days!

💧 *Two months, one goal. Ready to challenge yourself? This tracker will keep you moving forward, one week at a time.*

*https://shopunlocked.com/downloads/the-60-day-fund-builder-tracker/*

## 💡 Wanna Test Yourself?

You’ve learned the basics — now let’s put it to the test!

Take this quick quiz to check how much you’ve absorbed and how ready you are to apply it.

📲 **Scan the QR code** or **visit the link** to begin.

✍️ Whether you ace it or not, you’ll learn something valuable. Let’s go!

**Advanced Savings Strategies**

## Journal Prompt

**"What has stopped me from saving before—and what changes today?"**

Write 1 page on the emotions, habits, and beliefs that have blocked your progress—and the new mindset you're choosing now.

## Affirmations to Build Your Safety Net

- "I deserve to feel secure."
- "Saving is a gift to my future self."
- "I am building stability one dollar at a time."
- "I will not be caught off guard again."

*Funny but true: "My emergency fund isn't big yet, but at least it exists."*

## Visual Page: Emergency Fund Thermometer

Draw a thermometer and fill it up as you save. Break it into small goals ($50, $100, etc.). Color in as you fill up your fund

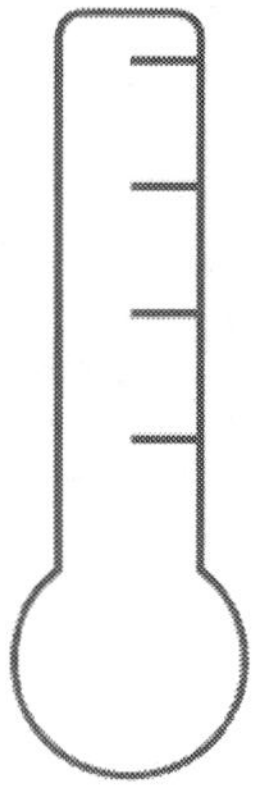

🌡 *Watch it grow. Fill in your thermometer as you build your emergency fund—each line brings you closer to peace of mind.*

*https://shopunlocked.com/downloads/emergency-fund-thermometer/*

### What's Next?

Now that you've built your financial cushion, it's time to explore the world of **credit**—how to use it, not fear it, and how it can become a tool (not a trap).

Coming up in Chapter 5: "Understand & Master Your Credit Score."

This page is left intentionally blank

CHAPTER 5

# Understand & Master Your Credit Score

*"Your credit doesn't define you, but it can shape your future. Learn it. Master it. Use it to your advantage."*

## What Is Credit, Really?

Let's make it simple:
**Credit** is your reputation with money.

When you borrow money (a loan, a credit card, financing a car), lenders want to know if they can trust you to pay it back. Your **credit score** is their way of deciding that. It's a number that says: *"Can this person be trusted with money?"*

> 🧠 *Think of it as your financial trust score. It tells the world how dependable you are when money is on the line.*

### Real-Life Comparison

Imagine two friends, Jada and Mike. Both apply for a phone plan. Jada has a 720 credit score—approved instantly. Mike has no credit history—he needs to pay a $500 deposit. Same phone. Different outcomes.

## Why It Matters

Even if you don't use credit now, your credit score affects:

- Renting an apartment
- Getting a cellphone plan
- Buying a car or home
- Getting a better job (some employers check credit!)
- Lowering your insurance premiums

Funny but true: "You might not care about credit, but landlords, banks, and jobs do!"

> 💡 *Peace of mind is easier to build when your credit isn't holding you back.*

## Connecting Credit to Your Savings Style

In Chapter 2, we explored different **savings styles**: the Automator, the Hustler, the Cash Stuffer, and the Round-Up Saver. Let's now connect these to your credit journey. Here's how your savings style can influence your credit—without going deep into credit management (that's for another book).

**If you're an Automator:**

Your bills and savings happen automatically—great! You can also **automate your credit card minimum payments** to never miss a due date. Even one late payment can hurt your score.

**If you're a Hustler:**

You're always making money on the side. Consider **using a credit card for specific purchases like gas or online ads**, then paying it off monthly. You'll build credit while building business.

**If you're a Cash Stuffer:**

You love seeing money in envelopes. Start using one labeled **"credit card payment"** to pay off small charges you make for planned spending. Don't fear cards—use them like tools.

**If you're a Round-Up Saver:**

You're tech-friendly and use apps. Some apps let you **pay bills or subscriptions with a credit card**, which helps build credit if you keep usage low. Monitor these expenses to stay in control.

> 🎯 *Each savings model gives you a natural strength. Now it's time to apply it to your credit, gently.*

## How Is Your Score Calculated?

Here are the 5 main factors:

| Factor | % of Score | What It Means |
|---|---|---|
| Payment History | 35% | Do you pay on time? Even $5 late can hurt. |
| Credit Utilization | 30% | Are you using too much of your available credit? |
| Credit Age | 15% | How long have your accounts been open? |
| Credit Mix | 10% | Do you have different types (card, loan, etc.)? |
| New Credit Inquiries | 10% | Are you applying for lots of credit at once? |

> ✨ *Think of your score like a report card for adults. 850 is an A+. 580 or below is an F.*

### Exercise: Credit Score Breakdown

Draw five boxes and label each with the above factors. Write 1 example of how you can improve each one.

| | |
|---|---|
| 1 | 2 |
| 3 | 4 |
| 5 | |

## In-Book Quiz: What's Your Credit Score IQ?

### True or False:

1. Paying your phone bill late hurts your credit.
2. Closing a credit card always improves your score.
3. Using more than 30% of your credit limit can drop your score.
4. Checking your own credit lowers your score.
5. Student loans affect your credit.

😳 *Answers: 1) False, unless it's reported. 2) False. 3) True. 4) False. 5) True.*

🔍 *Wanna see what's really behind that number? Use this visual to decode your score and take control.*

*https://shopunlocked.com/downloads/credit-score-breakdown/*

## Common Credit Mistakes

### 1. Maxing Out Cards

If your credit limit is $1,000, don't use more than $300 at a time.

### 2. Paying Late

Even one late payment can drop your score by 50+ points.

### 3. Not Having Credit

No credit history = no data = higher risk.

### 4. Co-signing Without Caution

You are legally responsible if the other person doesn't pay.

**Storytime: Carla's Mistake**

Carla co-signed for her cousin's car loan. He missed 3 payments. Carla's score dropped by 92 points. It took her 18 months to recover.

### Real-Life Story: Brian's 720 Miracle

Brian ignored his credit until he needed a car. His score? 524.

He got a secured credit card, paid every month, and never used more than 20% of the limit. He set up auto-pay and worked 1-on-1 with a Shopunlocked coach to learn.

In 14 months, his score hit 720. He got the car. And a lower interest rate. ✨

> *"Credit was the key that unlocked everything."*

### 💡 Real-Life Spotlight: Sarah's Credit Comeback

**"I didn't need magic—just the right steps."**

When Sarah joined the Shopunlocked coaching program, her credit score was stuck at **630**, and she felt stuck too. She had maxed out 3 credit cards, missed a few payments during the pandemic, and her limit hadn't increased in years.

"I was embarrassed," she says. "Every time I applied for credit, I got denied. I thought I was just bad with money."

But in her first coaching session, she learned how credit scores actually work—and how they can be *intentionally* repaired. She followed a **4-week credit reset plan**:

1. She paid down two cards below 30% utilization.
2. She changed her payment date to report early to the bureaus.
3. She set up autopay for the minimum on all accounts to avoid late payments.
4. She called her card issuers and requested a credit limit increase—two of them said yes!

By the end of the month, her score jumped from **630 to 701**, and she was approved for a **$3,000 increase** in total credit limits.

"I cried when I saw my score," Sarah said. "I felt powerful for the first time. Shopunlocked gave me the steps—and I took them." ✨

## Credit Do's and Don'ts (Simplified Edition)

☑ **DO:**

- Pay at least the minimum on time
- Keep utilization under 30%
- Check your credit report yearly (free at AnnualCreditReport.com)
- Ask for credit line increases after 6 months of good history

❌ **DON'T:**

- Open too many accounts fast
- Ignore your score
- Assume your score doesn't matter if you use cash only

> 🎯 *Use this list as your 1-page guide on the fridge or in your journal.*

## Worksheet: My Credit Snapshot

| Question | Your Answer |
| --- | --- |
| Do you have a credit score? | |
| Do you have at least 1 credit card? | |
| Do you pay bills on time? | |
| Are you using more than 30% of your limit? | |
| What is your credit goal in the next 12 months? | |

> 💡 *Tip: Write this again 6 months from now to track progress.*

## 6 Months Later :

| Question | Your Answer |
| --- | --- |
| Do you have a credit score? | |
| Do you have at least 1 credit card? | |
| Do you pay bills on time? | |
| Are you using more than 30% of your limit? | |
| What is your credit goal in the next 12 months? | |

## Exercise: Spot the Credit Triggers in Your Budget

Take out your Monthly Budget Worksheet from Chapter 2. Now go line by line and ask yourself:

- Can this expense be paid with a credit card?
- If yes, do I have a plan to pay it off on time?
- Does this bill report to credit bureaus (e.g., utilities, phone plans)?
- Is this a fixed or variable cost? Could automating it help me build credit?

### Instructions:

1. Highlight all items that **could** be linked to your credit use.
2. Add a ✔ next to items you already pay on time.
3. Circle any high-interest or recurring expense you could automate or pay down.

🧠 *This exercise helps you link daily money habits with long-term credit health—without diving into advanced credit strategy.*

________________________________________________

________________________________________________

________________________________________________

________________________________________________

________________________________________________

## Journal Prompt

**"If my credit could talk, what would it say about me? What do I want it to say by next year?"**

Write a full page reflecting on your habits, your fears, and your future.

✍ *This page will become your personal vow.*

## Affirmations to Rebuild & Empower

- "I am not my past mistakes."
- "I choose responsibility over avoidance."
- "I deserve access to opportunities."
- "Every on-time payment is a step toward freedom."

> *Funny but true: "Your credit score is like your ex—it remembers everything."*

___

___

___

**Visual: Credit Climb Tracker**

Draw a staircase from 500 to 850. Mark checkpoints: 580, 640, 680, 720, 750, 800.

Use one stair per milestone.

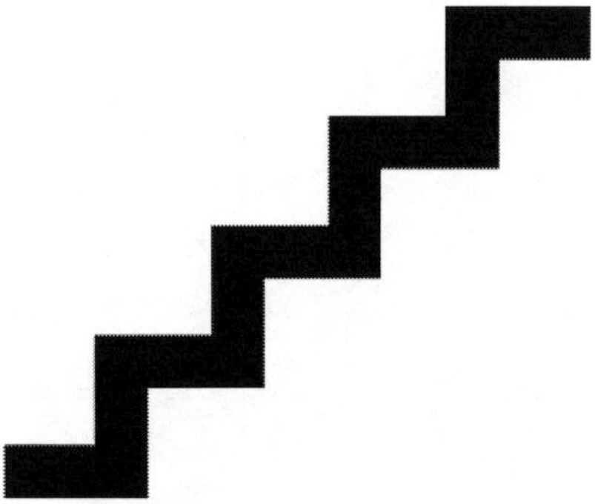

## Bonus: Resources You Can Trust (Ref: United States)

- AnnualCreditReport.com — free credit report
- Credit Karma — score tracking
- Shopunlocked.com — coaching, videos, support

---

### What's Next?

Now that you understand credit, let's talk about how to stay out of the trap: **debt.**

Coming up in Chapter 6: *"Break Free from the Debt Cycle."*

This page is left intentionally blank

CHAPTER 6

# Break Free from the Debt Cycle

*"Debt isn't just numbers. It's emotional weight. Let's start lifting it."*

## Why We Need to Talk About Debt

If you've ever felt like your paycheck is gone the second it lands — debt is probably involved. Credit cards. Student loans. Car payments. Buy-now-pay-later apps. It stacks up quietly until you're living in a cycle of paying for the past instead of planning for the future.

But here's what no one tells you:

**You're not lazy. You're not irresponsible. You're carrying a system that was built to keep you stuck.**

Debt feeds on guilt and delay. This chapter is your invitation to stop running from it and start facing it — with clarity, courage, and a plan.

## What Is Debt?

Debt is borrowed money — but it's also borrowed time. And time comes with a price: interest.

You borrowed money when you needed it. That's okay. Life happens. But now, debt is demanding to be repaid... plus extra. That "extra" is why so many people stay stuck.

Let's unpack the different types:

## ⚖️ Types of Debt (With Plain Truths)

| Type | Description | Good or Bad? |
|---|---|---|
| **Credit Cards** | High-interest revolving debt | ❌ Bad – unless paid in full monthly |
| **Student Loans** | Education-related debt | ⚠️ Mixed – helps earn more long-term |
| **Personal Loans** | Often used for emergencies or large purchases | ❌ Risky – easy to abuse |
| **Car Loans** | Financing a depreciating asset | ⚠️ Manageable – if car is essential |
| **Buy Now, Pay Later** | Apps like Klarna/Afterpay | ❌ Looks harmless, builds fast |
| **Mortgage** | Home loan that builds equity over time | ☑️ If payments are stable |
| **Line of Credit** | Flexible borrowing with lower interest | ⚠️ Dangerous if used like a paycheck |

## What Debt Feels Like

Debt is more than money. It's:

- The knot in your stomach when a bill hits
- The shame when you say "I'll catch up next month" — for the 6th month in a row
- The silence when you ignore a collections call

- The sting of feeling behind — even when you work hard every single day

This is your permission to stop blaming yourself. Debt is **not a moral failure**. It's a situation. And situations can change.

## 💡 The 50/30/20 Rule — and Why Debt Makes It Harder

We've talked about this rule :

- **50% of your income → Needs** (rent, food, bills)
- **30% → Wants** (fun, dining out, extras)
- **20% → Financial goals** (saving, investing, paying off debt)

That last 20% is where things get tricky — because it asks you to split your money between:

- **Building savings**
- **Paying off debt**

But when your emergency fund is low and your debt is high, how do you choose?

The truth? **You need both** — even if you can't do them at full speed right now.

### 💔 Debt vs. Savings: The Emotional Tug-of-War

This choice is personal. Emotional. Stressful. On one hand, debt is expensive — the longer it stays, the more it costs.

On the other hand, not having an emergency fund means **one surprise** can push you deeper into debt.

**Most people flip-flop:**

- Save $200 → Emergency → Use credit card
- Pay $200 on debt → Emergency → Take out loan

They stay trapped because they don't feel secure enough to focus on one direction.

## 💪 The Strategy: Save a Small Cushion, Then Hit Debt

Here's the plan that works for most people in your shoes:

**Step 1: Build a Starter Emergency Fund**

- Save **$500 to $1,000** as fast as you can.
- Hustle. Sell. Cut. Automate. Whatever it takes.
- This isn't your full emergency fund — it's just your buffer to stop going backward.

💡 *Think of it like putting on your seatbelt before you hit the road.*

**Step 2: Tackle Debt with Focus**

- Once your cushion is ready, shift your energy to debt.
- Keep your emergency savings untouched unless it's truly necessary.

- This gives you mental space to attack debt without fear.

**Step 3: When Debt Shrinks, Savings Grows**

- As balances go down, redirect some of your freed-up payments to rebuild your savings.
- Eventually, you can work toward a full 3–6 month emergency fund.

💡 **Wanna Test Yourself?**

You've learned the basics — now let's put it to the test!

Take this quick quiz to check how much you've absorbed and how ready you are to apply it.

📲 **Scan the QR code** or **visit the link** to begin.

✍ Whether you ace it or not, you'll learn something valuable. Let's go!

**Leveraging Financial Management Tools**

### Real-Life Example: Melanie's $700 Cushion

Melanie had $4,200 in credit card debt and no savings. She used to try paying off $300/month, but then the car would break down or her child got sick — and she'd swipe the card again.

When she paused and saved her first $700 instead, something changed:

"I had breathing room. When the unexpected hit, I didn't reach for the card. That changed everything."

### Real-Life Spotlight: Jonathan's Turning Point

**"I thought I needed more money—turns out I needed a better system."**

Jonathan worked full-time in transportation and brought home decent pay. But every month, his paycheck disappeared almost as fast as it came in. Between minimum payments on 5 credit cards, two personal loans, and a small car note, he was shelling out over **$1,100/month** on debt alone. His credit score hovered at **645**, and his stress level was through the roof.

"I kept looking for side hustles because I thought the problem was income. But no matter how much I made, I never felt free."

That changed when Jonathan joined **Shopunlocked's Private Debt Elimination Coaching**. In Week 1, he completed a deep-dive intake and got a personal debt snapshot with interest rates, due dates, and payoff projections. By Week 2, his coach helped him pick the best **Method for his situation**, targeting high-interest balances first. They restructured his payments into a 4-month strategy.

But it wasn't just numbers.

"I had someone to check in with every week. Someone who reminded me this wasn't just math—it was mindset."

By Week 4, Jonathan had:

- Paid off his highest-interest card
- Reduced his monthly payments by **$420**
- Raised his credit score to **712**
- Gained the confidence to call and negotiate a better car loan rate

"I've never felt this in control of my future. Shopunlocked didn't just help me eliminate debt—they helped me rebuild belief in myself."

## 📌 Mindset Reset: You Can Do Both — Slowly

You don't have to choose between debt freedom and security. You can walk both paths at the same time:

- One is about *peace of mind today*

- One is about *freedom tomorrow*

Some months, you'll save more. Some months, you'll pay down more. What matters is that you stay aware, intentional, and in motion.

## ✨ Journal Prompt: Debt Without Shame

Write about a time when debt made you feel embarrassed or discouraged.

Then write down 3 things you've done right — even in the middle of financial stress.

Close with one thing you'll do this week to take back control — no guilt, just progress.

### ● Wait—Can My Credit Card Be My Emergency Fund?

Let's talk about something real. Once your credit card balance is **paid off**, it can feel like you suddenly have *money* again. And in a way — you do.

💳 A zero-balance card with a $2,000 limit **does** represent available credit. But here's the mindset shift:

**It's not your money. It's borrowed access.**

That said, if you're in between building your full emergency fund, a cleared credit card can serve as a **temporary emergency back-up** — not your primary safety net.

When It's Okay to Think of Credit as Backup Cash

If:

- You have **no savings yet**
- You've just **finished paying down your card**
- You're working on a **starter emergency fund** (first $500–$1,000)
- You've stopped using the card for everyday spending

...then yes, that credit limit can be **part of your emergency plan** — but it's like a fire extinguisher. You hope you never have to grab it.

The Golden Rule: Emergency Fund First, Credit Back-Up Second

Here's how to balance it:

1. Save your first $500–$1,000 in real cash.
2. Keep your cleared card in your back pocket for true emergencies only.
3. As you grow your cash savings, rely less and less on credit for security.

This lets you move from survival mode to real freedom — where emergencies don't turn into new debt.

📌 **Reminder:**

**A cleared credit card is not income.**

It's a tool — and tools are only helpful when used with discipline.

If you're not sure how to use that tool wisely, you're not alone. Most people were never taught the right way to manage credit limits, payment timing, or utilization rates.

That's why we created the **Credit Boost & Monitoring Course** at Shopunlocked — to give you a simple, step-by-step plan to use credit cards the smart way and never feel lost again.

Because once you know how it works, you can make it work for *you*.

**What's Next?**

In Chapter 7, we'll explore **how to protect the money you're working so hard to build** — from scams, leaks, and bad habits. This is where your new systems start clicking into place.

Let's keep growing.

This page is left intentionally blank

CHAPTER 7

# Protect Your Money

> *"It's not just what you earn — it's what you keep that builds real wealth."*

## Why Protection Matters

After all the effort you've put into budgeting, saving, and getting out of debt, the last thing you want is to let your progress slip away. That's what this chapter is about — protecting the money you've worked so hard to manage. Not just from scams, but from subscriptions, bad habits, and emotional spending. Let's lock in your progress.

## Leaks That Drain Your Wallet

The little things can cost you big over time. $9.99 here, $14.99 there — that's how financial leaks work. They sneak up on you and eat away at your hard work.

**Common leaks:**

- Subscriptions you forgot to cancel

- Auto-renewals for apps, courses, or streaming
- ATM or overdraft fees
- Late fees from missed due dates
- Emotional spending after a bad day

📌 Action step: Review your last 3 months of bank and credit card statements. Highlight every charge that wasn't planned or necessary.

## Scam-Proof Your Wallet

Financial scams are on the rise — especially in immigrant communities and among young adults. Scammers prey on urgency, fear, and trust.

**❌ Red flags to watch for:**

- Unsolicited calls asking for money or gift cards
- Texts saying 'your account is locked' — always verify
- Fake investment promises ('Double your money in 5 days!')
- Pressure to act fast, especially through Zelle, Cash App, or wire transfer

📌 Action step: Set up two-factor authentication on all financial apps. Never send money without double-checking the source.

## Protect Your Digital Finances

Your financial data is just as important as your physical money. Here's how to protect it:

- Use unique passwords for bank and payment apps
- Avoid using public Wi-Fi to access banking
- Get alerts for large purchases or low balances
- Turn on notifications for failed login attempts

> 📌 *Action step: Review your security settings on all financial platforms and apps. Update your passwords today.*

This page is left intentionally blank

CHAPTER 8

# Multiply Your Money – A Beginner's Guide to Investing

> *"You've done the hard work. Now let your money do some of it too."*

## A Natural Next Step

If you've made it this far, pause—breathe—and recognize what you've just done.

You didn't just read a book.

You confronted your habits, rewrote your money story, built your first real budget, took control of your savings, created a safety net, faced your debt, and learned how to protect your credit and peace of mind.

That is transformational work.

And now comes the next step.

Not a leap into risk, but a quiet, steady decision to grow what you've worked so hard to protect.

This chapter isn't about getting rich overnight. It's about shifting from *survival mode* to *strategy mode.*

Because investing isn't just for Wall Street types or people with six-figure incomes.

It's for people like you—people who've learned to manage, save, and think long term.

You're ready. Let's begin.

## Saving vs. Investing

Saving is putting money in a safe place for short-term goals or emergencies. Investing is buying something that can grow in value over time.

Think of saving as security. Think of investing as growth. You need both.

## Start Small

You don't need thousands of dollars to invest. You can start with just $10 using apps like Acorns, Fidelity, Shopunlocked or Charles Schwab. Fractional shares allow you to buy a piece of stock without paying the full price. Small, consistent steps matter.

## Where Can I Start Investing?

| Type | What It Is | Risk Level | Good For Beginners? |
|---|---|---|---|
| Savings Account | Very low return, very safe | Very Low | ☑ |
| CDs | Lock money for set time to earn interest | Low | ☑ |
| ETFs | Bundles of stocks that spread out risk | Medium | |
| Individual Stocks | Shares of one company | High | ⚠ Not at first |
| Crypto | Digital currency, very volatile | Very High | ✖ |
| Private Lending (Shopunlocked) | Lend $1,000+ as a micro-investor via Shopunlocked | Medium | ☑ If guided |

### 💡 MONEY HABITS THAT STICK

> *"You don't need a big win. You need small wins, done consistently."*

The little things you do daily shape your financial future. Wealth is built from the ground up—starting with routines that become second nature.

### ☑ The 1% Rule

**What it means:**

Instead of trying to overhaul your entire financial life overnight, just aim to get *1% better* each day. That small improvement might feel invisible now—but over time, it compounds into massive growth.

**Real-Life Example:**

Jasmine was always behind on bills and avoided looking at her bank account. Instead of setting a big, intimidating financial goal, she started with one tiny change: reviewing her bank app for 60 seconds each morning.

After two weeks, she added a habit of transferring $1 a day to savings. After a month, she raised it to $5.

Six months later? She had $600 in savings—without ever "feeling" the pinch. Her mindset had also completely shifted. ✨

**Mini Challenge:**

What's one thing you can improve today by 1%?

- Spend 1% less on food?
- Add $1/day to savings?
- Learn one money term per day?

## 🔗 Habit Stacking

**What it means:**

Connect your new money habit to something you *already* do daily. That way, it becomes part of your routine—effortlessly.

**Formula:**

"After I [existing habit], I will [new money habit]."

### Real-Life Example:

David always made coffee at 7 AM. He decided to stack a 2-minute review of his expense tracker right after pouring his coffee.

Now, "coffee + review spending" go hand-in-hand—no mental friction.

### Other examples:

- After brushing teeth at night → check savings app.
- After eating lunch → write down any unexpected spending.
- After logging into work → glance at credit card balance.

**Mini Challenge:**

Write down 1 existing habit. Then link it to 1 small money task.

Example:

"After I brush my teeth, I will transfer $2 to savings."

> 💡 *You can totally write in here. Scribble away like it's your personal money journal!*

______________________________________________

______________________________________________

______________________________________________

______________________________________________

## 🔁 Money Rituals

💡 You can totally write in here. Scribble away like it's your personal money journal!

### What it means:

Create consistent weekly or monthly check-ins with your money—just like meal prep, laundry, or self-care. This builds *trust* and *clarity* around your finances.

**Real-Life Example:**

Every Sunday evening, Marc and his wife sit down for 20 minutes. They call it their "Money & Mimosas" ritual. They review:

- What they spent last week
- What bills are due
- What they're saving toward
- They even play a short "money wins" game: Who saved the most? Who skipped impulse buys?

Even if their week was tight, the ritual makes them feel in control.

**Mini Challenge:**

Pick your ritual day and time. Try one of these:

- **Weekly:** Sunday Money Hour
- **Monthly:** First-of-the-month Reflection
- **Quarterly:** Financial Reset (budget + goals + review)

These aren't just habits. They're new identity anchors.

☞ When you act like a person who respects money—even in small, quiet ways—you *become* that person.

## ✍ Worksheet: Your Weekly Money Routine

Create a 7-day grid to track habits like budgeting, no-spend days, or reviewing bills. Use this tracker to build consistency with your money routines. Check off each task as you complete it throughout the week.

### ✍ Example

| | M | T | W | TH | F | S | SU |
|---|---|---|---|---|---|---|---|
| Check Bank Account | ☐ | ☐ | ☐ | ☐ | ☐ | ☐ | ☐ |
| Log Expenses | ☐ | ☐ | ☐ | ☐ | ☐ | ☐ | ☐ |
| Transfer to Savings | ☐ | ☐ | ☐ | ☐ | ☐ | ☐ | ☐ |
| No-Spend Day | ☐ | ☐ | ☐ | ☐ | ☐ | ☐ | ☐ |
| Review Budget | ☐ | ☐ | ☐ | ☐ | ☐ | ☐ | ☐ |
| Financial Podcast | ☐ | ☐ | ☐ | ☐ | ☐ | ☐ | ☐ |
| Set Weekly Goals | ☐ | ☐ | ☐ | ☐ | ☐ | ☐ | ☐ |

## ☑ Quiz: Are Your Habits Helping or Hurting?

- Do you review your budget at least once a week?
- Do you automate savings?
- Do you track impulsive purchases?

Mostly YES = Solid Habits | Mostly NO = Time to reset

🧘 *Money peace starts with routines. Use this printable grid to turn chaos into calm—just a few minutes a day.*

*https://shopunlocked.com/downloads/money-routine/*

## 🔥 STUFF YOU NEED TO STOP BUYING (AND WHAT TO BUY INSTEAD)

- Daily takeout → Cook 2x a week & freeze meals
- Cable TV → Netflix or a streaming bundle
- Designer bags → Invest in ETFs or business tools

### ✍️ Worksheet: Your Smart Spending Plan

List 5 recent purchases:

Purchase 1: ______________________________________

Purchase 2: ______________________________________

Purchase 3: ______________________________________

Purchase 4: ______________________________________

Purchase 5: ______________________________________

## Was it worth it?

What's a smarter substitute?

## 🗨 SHARE THE JOURNEY

Money isn't just personal—it's relational. Involve your partner, kids, or biz team.

- Use "we" language, not blame.
- Be honest: 'This is where we are. This is where we want to be.'

---

---

## ✍ Worksheet: Money Conversations Script

**Because talking about money shouldn't feel like a fight or a secret.**

Most people were never taught *how* to talk about money—so they either avoid it or argue about it. This worksheet helps you start respectful, real conversations with people who matter.

---

---

---

---

---

---

---

### 🗨 Situation 1: Wife Talking to Husband

**Goal:** Teamwork, transparency, shared goals

**Sample Starters:**

- "Can we check in on our money goals this weekend? Just 15 minutes."
- "What's one thing we could save for that excites us both?"
- "I noticed our grocery bill went up. Want to brainstorm ways to save together?"

**What NOT to say:**

- "You're spending too much again."
- "Why can't you just budget like I do?"

**Mini Challenge:** Schedule a "Money & Chill" night once a month—snacks + financial check-in.

### 💬 Situation 2: Husband Talking to Wife

**Goal:** Openness, avoiding tension, inviting partnership

**Sample Starters:**

- "Hey love, I've been thinking about our credit card balance. Want to figure out a plan together?"
- "What's one financial habit we could both improve this month?"
- "What's a money goal you've been thinking about but haven't said out loud?"

> **Respect tip:** *Always invite, never demand. Frame money as a shared responsibility.*

### 🗨 Situation 3: Parent Talking to a Young Child

**Goal:** Introduce money early, normalize healthy habits

**Sample Starters:**

- "Let's play store! You get $5 to spend, and $1 to save."
- "Why do you think we have a savings jar at home?"
- "When you get birthday money, what do you want to do with it—save, spend, or share?"

> **Keep it fun:** *Use play, stickers, and rewards to teach saving and decision-making.*

### 🗨 Situation 4: Parent Talking to a Teenager

**Goal:** Build trust, explain real-life money consequences

**Sample Starters:**

- "What would you do if you had $100 right now?"
- "I want to show you how I budget this month's bills. Want to learn with me?"
- "Do you want help setting up a debit card or savings account?"

**Avoid:**

- Lectures without examples
- Guilt-based language ("When I was your age...")

> **Pro Tip:** *Let them manage a small monthly budget (even if it's $20) and guide—not control—their choices.*

### 🗨 Situation 5: Work Environment (Business Partner or Team)

**Goal:** Set clear roles, avoid resentment, align on goals

### Sample Starters:

- "Let's set a monthly financial check-in so we're both in the loop."
- "Do you feel clear about how profits are being tracked and split?"
- "What's one expense we should eliminate or re-evaluate this month?"

### Bonus Tip for Entrepreneurs:

Use shared tools like Google Sheets, Notion, or Wave Apps to keep everything visible and organized.

### 📝 DIY Prompts for Any Conversation

Write your answers below, then use them in a real conversation this week.

1. A goal I'd like to talk about is:
2. Something I've been nervous to ask about:
3. A win I'm proud of lately:
4. A habit I'd like us to build together:

# 🎯 Your Next Steps: Credit,Debt & Investing preview

You've just scratched the surface.

✔ The Credit Book – Learn how to master your credit score.

✔ The Debt-Free Book – Crush debt, one move at a time.

✔ The Investing Starter Kit – Learn to grow your money safely.

📥 Signup at shopunlocked.com/contact-us/ to get alerts + Gifts

### 💡 Wanna Test Yourself?

You've learned the basics — now let's put it to the test!

Take this quick quiz to check how much you've absorbed and how ready you are to apply it.

📲 **Scan the QR code** or **visit the link** to begin.

✍ Whether you ace it or not, you'll learn something valuable. Let's go!

## Setting Financial Goals for the Future

# 📓 Your Financial Blueprint Bring It All Together

Let's recap your journey:

1. Understand your money story
2. Learn money fundamentals
3. Build a real-life budget
4. Start saving with a strategy
5. Build an emergency fund
6. Protect your money from leaks and scams
7. Break free from debt
8. Begin investing wisely

Now create your custom blueprint. Use this checklist:

- ☐ Budget built and updated monthly
- ☐ Emergency fund at $500, aiming for 3–6 months
- ☐ Debt plan in motion or complete
- ☐ Auto-savings set up
- ☐ First $10–$100 invested (Shopunlocked or ETF)
- ☐ Logins secured, alerts set, and mindset reset

**You did it ✅ — and this is just the beginning.**

# THANK YOU

To my children — my heartbeats, my light, my reason. This book exists because you reminded me daily what purpose feels like. Your strength, patience, and unconditional love have been the greatest wealth I've ever known. Every late-night writing, every quiet tear of doubt, and every step forward was fueled by the desire to be the kind of example you deserve.

To YOU, dear reader — thank you for allowing me into your story. You didn't have to pick up this book. But you did. You chose to trust a stranger with something deeply personal — your money, your hope, your future. I don't take that lightly.

If this book has helped you — even just a little — please know my gratitude is deep and real. I wrote this with you in mind. With your family in mind. With your dreams in mind.

If you ever feel alone on this journey, I want you to remember: I've been where you are. And if you want someone walking with you — not above you, not in front of you — just beside you, guiding you — I'd be honored to be your coach.

From the bottom of my heart, thank you.

To God be the glory — always and forever.

rg.
REGINE GODEFROY
AUTHOR

## 📝 Journal Reflection

This page was left blank intentionally—for your thoughts, your wins, your breakthroughs.

**This is where the shift began.** *Reflect on what felt different as you worked through this book.*

## 📝 Journal Reflection

This page was left blank intentionally—for your thoughts, your wins, your breakthroughs.

*What money habit am I proud of today?*

### 📝 Journal Reflection

This page was left blank intentionally—for your thoughts, your wins, your breakthroughs.

**I didn't just read this — I lived it.** *Write down a real change you made.*

## 📝 Journal Reflection

This page was left blank intentionally—for your thoughts, your wins, your breakthroughs.

**Credit doesn't define me, but I'm ready to master it.**

## 📝 Journal Reflection

This page was left blank intentionally—for your thoughts, your wins, your breakthroughs.

**Debt used to scare me. Now I'm building a plan.**

### 📝 Journal Reflection

This page was left blank intentionally—for your thoughts, your wins, your breakthroughs.

*What would financial peace feel like every morning?*

## 📝 Journal Reflection

This page was left blank intentionally—for your thoughts, your wins, your breakthroughs.

If I had an extra $1,000 right now, what would I do with it? *Let's transition together towards investing*

## 📝 Journal Reflection

This page was left blank intentionally—for your thoughts, your wins, your breakthroughs.

**I deserve overflow, not survival.** *Let this be a reminder you are not here to just get by.*

## 📝 Journal Reflection

This page was left blank intentionally—for your thoughts, your wins, your breakthroughs.

*What does 'wealth' look like in my life — on my terms?*

### 📝 Journal Reflection

This page was left blank intentionally—for your thoughts, your wins, your breakthroughs.

*The best money decision I've made so far is...*

### 📝 Journal Reflection

This page was left blank intentionally—for your thoughts, your wins, your breakthroughs.

**I didn't grow up with this knowledge — but I'm passing it on.** *Legacy-focused, let's break generational cycles together.*

## 📝 Journal Reflection

This page was left blank intentionally—for your thoughts, your wins, your breakthroughs.

**Investing is not out of reach. I just needed the right guide.**

## 📝 Journal Reflection

This page was left blank intentionally—for your thoughts, your wins, your breakthroughs.

**The old me was scared to look at my finances. The new me?**

# 🕮 About the Author

**Regine Godefroy** is a passionate business coach, entrepreneur, and educator. With over 30 years of lived experience, she has empowered thousands of immigrants and first-generation learners to take control of their finances, launch their side hustles, and build lasting wealth—without needing a fancy degree.

A devoted mother and faith-driven leader, Regine is the founder of ShopUnlocked.com, where she shares powerful lessons through courses, coaching, and community support. Her mission is simple: demystify money, empower action, and help everyday people win.

🗨 **You can book Regine for 1-on-1 coaching or find her resources at Shopunlocked.com**

This page is left intentionally blank

Made in the USA
Monee, IL
12 November 2026

d77d7558-25ea-42da-a192-336d5cd83191R01